A BOOK F(

...HOW TO TALK TO YOUR MASTER

Written by Stuart Ryan
Illustrated by Richard Lowdell

Nightingale Press
an imprint of Wimbledon Publishing Company
LONDON

Copyright © 2001
Illustrations © 2001 WPC

First published in Great Britain
by Wimbledon Publishing Co. Ltd
London P.O. Box 9779 SW19 7ZG
All rights reserved

ISBN: 1903222 26 5

Produced in Great Britain
Printed and bound in Hungary

Introduction

Boys, we have come a long way since we were wolves roaming the forests. In this century we dogs have achieved more than in any other. We have flown into space - and who did our masters trust first to send into this dangerous uncharted territory, eh? We have been accepted into the police force (although there is still an alarmingly low acceptance of black labradors) and again they trust us in the most dangerous of circumstances - if there is a bomb-scare, we go in first, right? Yet we are still lacking something.

Beyond all these great achievements we are still not really communicating - we are still misunderstood, ignored or viewed as entertainment. It is time to adjust, time to face up to facts. In this age of technology, communication is the key. I hear my owner talking about the 'unternit' , 'e-moil', 'the tallyphine'. They are reaching out to one another more than ever and now it is time to follow suit. Boys, I am talkin' 'bout a revolution. Stick with me and learn how to reach out and touch your master.

CATS

Inspiration comes from the strangest places - in this case it glides in through a hole in the back door. Kitty seems to be particularly adept at communicating with our owners, to the point where, if we are not careful, she receives their undivided attention.

However, friends, it is possible to steal that moggy's thunder just by emulating her behaviour. Firstly, the entrance: Glide in with poise and grace.

Next, sight the target. Do not bound up, tongue out and drooling, instead adopt an air of aloof cool. Don't bark, try a low whine instead - softer sounds are easier on our owners' ears and always work for kitty!

She has worked out that physical contact is the winner - see how she poises on our masters' head? When the time is right, and your owner least expects it, soar through the air and aim for the bonce. Once there, balance is the key. I must admit that I haven't tried this myself, but if the cat can do it, I'm sure we can!

Anyhow, there is clearly room to improve upon kitty's fawning - if she were making a good job of things she wouldn't be thrown out each night, would she?

BARKING

Ah, the sound of music. At the heart of all communication is the voice. If you really want to be recognised in this world you have to shout out! It really does work! Try it and see what I mean - the louder you shout, the louder your owner will shout back at you! He will give you words of encouragement: "SHUT UP! SHUT UP!!!", and the louder you bark, the greater his enthusiasm will be: "AAARGH! For God's sake!! SHUT UP!!!!" Now is that some kind of connection or what!

DIETING

"Dieting"? They are always talking about this thing called "dieting " - especially when they seem reluctant to eat. So why are they surprised that we snarl if they approach our dinner? I mean, come on boys - we are doing them a favour; I'm sure that if we turned away for an instant they would be down on all fours gobbling on our Chicken and Rabbit Pedigree Chum from the bowl marked 'Dog.' (Incidentally who is 'Dog?' and why do we always get his bowl?) So, communicate this idea to them by a menacing growl - with our help they will stick to those "diets!"

FENG SHUI

This thing called "Feng Shui" - the order of things. Our owners are so influenced by New Age lifestyles and philosophies, yet they don't know how best to exploit them. How many times have you seen your owner trip over a slipper he has left at the top of the stairs? Evidently we need to communicate the correct way of feng shui. First, find the object that needs to be moved. It is normally a slipper. (Actually, I've only ever moved slippers). Anyway, once you have found the offending object, the feng shui can commence. Move the object from the house and out to the garden. Next, dig a large hole and put the slipper in it. Cover the hole and there you go boys, order restored.

Physical Contact

As we all know, physical contact is a staple of any effective relationship. You can communicate so much with a subtle gesture. Watch our owners - they use physical contact to communicate their love, be it through a gentle caress or a manly hug. Clearly the realm of touch is not confined to them. See how close they become when they hug? We can do this too. The best place to hug your owner is around their leg. First, time your jump effectively. Then, when you are on two legs, wrap your front paws tightly around that manly thigh and proceed to hug it with a gentle forwards and backwards motion. You know what? It feels good doesn't it? Usually your owner will reciprocate this feeling by shaking his leg in time with yours and offering words of encouragement like "Get off!" and "Eurgh, what a mess!"

CURRENT AFFAIRS

It is becoming increasingly important to demonstrate an interest in current affairs - if we get left behind in this area how can we possibly hope to communicate with our owners? So, as soon as the newspaper arrives through the letterbox make sure that you are there first! Then, show your interest by grabbing it, running like hell and hiding under the bed! Your owner will chase you, but only because the news is so important to him. How wonderful then, for him to know that it is equally important to you! It gets better though - I always hear him talk of "digesting" the news - so make sure you eat that paper before he gets a chance to do so! He may be in a huff because he has to buy a new one - but this all pays off when you both finally get to sit down together and share your appreciation of the day's events.

FINE FOOD

Our owners seem to labour under the misapprehension that we are simple creatures who do not appreciate the finer things in life. Obviously we have to prove them wrong and demonstrate that we are sophisticated and cultured. I would suggest first conveying an interest in fine food: whenever you see your owner clasping an item of fine cuisine you must show him how dedicated to his interest you are. Now I have observed that this kind of food always comes in small portions so obviously he is not going to be keen to give much away. Therefore, as soon as he turns his back, eat all you can! SCOFF! SCOFF! SCOFF!!! Ignore his protestations - it is essential that he sees how interested you are! And remember, the more you eat, the more interested you will appear!

Beyond fine food you must be able to demonstrate a knowledge of fine beverages. Interestingly, when drinking that red liquid our owners mimic canine drinking techniques by spitting out half of the drink. With our large slobbering lips we are perfectly designed to show them that we know how to taste fine beverages too! Take a big gulp from the bowl in the bathroom (the one that isn't marked "dog") and you will see how it comes out naturally. Show your owners, share the experience with them, they will be impressed. Slobber away - fine water deserves appreciation!
Savour the taste, particularly the blue water from the bathroom bowl!

Personal Grooming

The 'New man' needs a 'New dog'. Personal grooming is essential if we are to reflect well on our owners. Now it is not easy I know - I mean, our owner will go out and buy a "new coat", something we never get the chance to do. And then he has all those styling products, some of which taste better than others...

I also understand that the ladies don't like facial hair. Again, nothing we can do about that, so we are going to have to rely on natural resources. I have seen our female owners commonly applying a "mud pack". Well, boys, I think we all know that there is no problem with obtaining a source of mud! When in the garden roll around in this most beautiful of substances, cake yourself in it and feel its cooling, exfoliating properties. Your owner will be impressed and shouts of encouragement such as "Stop it! You're filthy!" are to be expected. From here you need a relaxing soak so head over to the pond and take a dip. By now your beauty routine is nearly over. The final stage is for your owner to take you into the "rain machine" where the process of personal grooming is completed.

What I can't understand is why our owners skip the first two stages and head straight for the soaking?

THE ALARM CLOCK

The incessant moaning when they oversleep. Yes, fellas - we've all heard that one time and time again. It is essential to convey a sense of efficiency and energy to your owner. The alarm clock is no longer a valid weapon in his fight against sleep. Our solution? As soon as dawn cracks, fill your dribblers with as much water as they can leak and make your way upstairs. When you sight your groggy owner begin the approach, initially with stealth, then with a sudden burst of speed. At the crucial moment deposit that cool, refreshing water on your owner's face. Believe me it works! Haven't you noticed they love nothing more than an invigorating cold shower first thing in the morning!

DOMESTIC HELP

We are far more than cuddly creatures simply around to amuse and protect our owners. It is important to know all our functions. Watch your female owner and you will see that she is invariably rushed off her feet. A dirty house, food all over the place, toddlers with jam smeared lips. Well fellas, this is where we can perform the task of domestic help. First, the bathroom. Look at that toilet! Would you be happy drinking from that? I thought not - lick that bowl until it sparkles! And that sticky floor? Again, lick until that sweet stickiness has totally gone! Some floors are harder than others to clean. The carpet is particularly stubborn to licking and slobber. However I think I know the solution. Have you seen how our owner often pushes that machine across the carpet? Well, if you can copy that motion you should be able to drag all the dirt away with you. So, squat and drag chums and watch that dust fly!

And the kitchen - those left-overs on the table? Jump, eat and clean my boys! Just view all that food on the table (and maybe the floor) as your reward for a good deed. Mum certainly doesn't have time to clean all that jam and honey from toddlers' lips. So lick and lick again! You are doing a very good deed (and a sweet-tasting one at that) as well as making sure that junior is well-groomed and presentable.

Digging Holes

"Landscape gardening" I think that's human for digging holes. I once watched my owner spend days digging a lily-filled green-watered bathing pool for me. When it was finished he staggered back into the house clutching his back and moaning. After he had done all this work for my bathing pleasure I realised it was only fitting that we dogs help out with such labours. So look around your garden and try and anticipate where the work needs to be carried out next. Those plants? Winter is coming and they are going to die with all that cold weather! So clear them now - dig away and, if it is necessary to complete the job, EAT THEM!!

Our owners haven't got time in their busy schedules to clear away all that rubbish so dispose of it yourselves. And try and figure out where the next bathing pool is going to go - it is never too early to start on a new job and imagine their delight when they see the headway you have made! We can also contribute to the overall appearance of the garden. I have seen my owners dig a hole, insert something called "apple tree seeds" A few months later there is an apple tree full of juicy fruit! Well, I think we can do the same. Dig a deep, deep hole and drop a "bone seed" in there. I don't know how long they take to grow but I am guessing that in a few years I am going to be looking at a few well-stocked bone trees! Our owners will certainly be glad that we are contributing to the family wellbeing!

Children

"Mini owners." It is important to foster a good relationship with children as they are the owners of the future. Every bark, every slobber will be remembered in years to come. And one day one of my descendants may be digging and slobbering for one of these children. So, remember that children are impressionable creatures. It is often a good idea to try out all the tactics described before on children - this way they will be used to us by the time they reach late middle age. This includes physical contact and sports, as I have demonstrated. You will notice actually that children are far more receptive - their resistance is always much lower than that of adults!

VISITORS

As guardians of the gate we have that rare privilege of being the first point of contact for visitors. It is therefore important that we create the right impression - remember, boys, at this stage we are the representative for the family. So, it is essential to communicate with every visitor that tries to get through that gate.

First, signal their arrival with a hearty bark. In fact don't stop barking, even when your owner has judged them suitable to enter the threshold - it is important that they feel welcome.

Next check them out thoroughly - your owner's judgement cannot always be trusted. Smell them all over (ignore any resistance - this is an essential part of the security screening process.) Then lick them and see if you recognise the taste. If anything seems amiss it is probably wise at this point to take a playful nip - if there is a problem this will bring your master to his senses.

If, however, the visitors are judged to taste friendly they may be allowed to proceed to the next stage - the hallway. Remember your manners and offer to take their coat, hat, shoes, newspaper or anything else you can fit into your mouth. The further away you take it, the longer they will stay, as a game of hide and seek ensues. In fact if you bury it in the garden they may even stay the whole weekend! By this point the pleasantries will be over and the adults will be wanting to engage in mature discussion so do your best to drag the children away. If they fit in your mouth all the better. And if you can bury them better still.

You know when you have successfully welcomed the visitors because you will be rewarded with a biscuit and the peace and quiet that being locked in the kitchen provides. And if you have behaved especially well you can have the privilege of chasing them away.

THE GARDEN

Right fellas, listen carefully: The garden is a very good place for making a connection with your owner. Get them outside and they will really feel in touch with nature - remember boys, we too are a part of nature. Watch them carefully, monitor their behaviour and pretty soon you will see patterns emerging which you can copy. See the way they pour water on the plants - well, I think that one's obvious... And the way they caress them - again, no problem...

Plants require delicate attention so we should do all we can to maintain the fragile beauty of the garden. The good thing about the garden is it gives us an opportunity to see how our masters have taken on board some of our ways and skills. You've seen them spread manure on the cabbage patch? Well looks like we've influenced them somewhere along the way!

WALKS

Take the lead, literally. Getting out and about is a good way of introducing your master to your favourite places. He doesn't have any idea of where he is going so it is important that you lead confidently. Water some trees along the way - he will appreciate your continued interest in nature even beyond the confines of the garden. Take him through those puddles and swamps and don't worry about getting your paws muddy. Share those secret nooks and crannies in the forest, take him through your favourite stream. If he knows our favourite places then he will understand us better. Don't worry about his seeming reluctance to follow you through the bog - like any guest he is just uncomfortable in new surroundings.

SPORTS

Our owners are sports mad - have you noticed how competitive they get? Personally I think the only sports worth playing are 'chase the stick' or 'speed digging'. However, they do not rise to such sophistication and most of the time seem content to kick a ball from one end of the field to another (what is the point in that?!!). Anyway, it is important that we show our willingness to take part in such trials and so at the first opportunity get involved in this strange game! Now it is very easy to beat them all - the objective seems to be to destroy the ball, which is why they kick and punch at it with such vigour. All you need to do is pick the thing up in your mouth, bite hard and, hey presto, you've won! Once you have done this, your owner will give a defeated sigh and vacate the playing field, leaving you to enjoy that chewy, rubbery taste. But what I can't figure out is why, having seen us win like this so many times, they still persist in trying to break the ball with their feet and hands. Silly people. Still, you have to admire their tenacity.

LATE NIGHT SECURITY

Being a dog isn't all fun and games, oh no. There are prowlers out there who want to get into our safe abode and maybe even harm our owners. Every now and then you must play the role of Guard Dog. Our owners think they are safe with the "Burglar box" stuck on the side of the house, but, really, what good is that thing? How often do you hear it sound the alert? A squeak every couple of months, perhaps? Not the most reliable guard. So, it's up to us to bark! Bark at the slightest sound, fellas! We all know that a good bark will scare away even the most thuggish villain. And what's more, once your owner has been stirred from his deepest sleep - he will almost certainly have to come down to see what a good job you are doing!

THE POSTMAN

Every morning a sinister figure in blue strolls down the driveway, sticks his hand through the letterbox and delivers such evil that our owners always moan with despair when they look at it - "Oh no, not another bill!". Well, as with everything else we must protect our owner's interests. So, when you hear those clumping footsteps, let the barking commence! You have to hand it to postie, though - he is certainly brave and always continues his advance with great courage. You even have to admire his battle cry: "Aargh! Sod off you nippy little bastard!" Even so, when that hand comes through the door BITE! BITE! BITE!!! That will teach him! And when he has dropped the mail, chew it beyond all recognition so our owners don't have to face the pain of reading it!

Conclusion

Well fellas, hopefully this little guide will have given you some insight into how we can move up the evolutionary chain to become Number 1. All that stands in our way are those pesky dolphins. As for our owners, it is a shame to see them lingering so low, but at least we are there to look after them. You really think someone would write a book telling them how to communicate with us...